Discovering Religions

SIKHISM

Sue Penney

RSVP

**RAINTREE
STECK-VAUGHN**
P U B L I S H E R S
The Steck-Vaughn Company

Austin, Texas

Published by Raintree Steck-Vaughn Publishers, an imprint of Steck-Vaughn Company.

Library of Congress Cataloging-in-Publication Data

Penney, Sue.

Sikhism / Sue Penney.

p. cm. — (Discovering religions)

Includes index.

Summary: Explores the origins, history, teachings, and celebrations of Sikhism.

ISBN 0-8172-4398-4

1. Sikhism—Juvenile literature. [1. Sikhism.]

I. Title. II. Series.

BL2018.P46 1997

294.6—dc20 96-12379

CIP

AC

Religious Studies consultants: W. Owen Cole and Steven L. Ware (Drew University)

Thanks are due to Professor Bakhshish Singh for reading and advising on the manuscript.

Designed by Visual Image
Typeset by Tom Fenton Studio
Cover design by Amy Atkinson
Printed in Great Britain by Bath Press Colourbooks, Glasgow
1 2 3 4 5 6 7 8 9 WO 99 98 97 96

Acknowledgments

The publishers would like to thank the following for permission to reproduce photographs:

Cover photograph by Ann and Bury Peerless.

Andes Press Agency pp. 11, 21, 28, 44; Mohamed Ansar/Impact Photos p. 23; Circa Photo Library pp. 10, 42, 43; Mary Evans Picture Library p. 25; Sally and Richard Greenhill pp. 9, 36; Robert Harding Picture Library p. 26; Judy Harrison/Format Partners pp. 12 (top), 33, 39; The Hutchison Library pp. 6, 12 (below), 18, 22, 40, 41, 47; Christine Osborne Pictures pp. 13, 14, 32, 34, 35, 38, 46; Ann and Bury Peerless pp. 17, 19, 27, 29, 30, 31; Peter Sanders pp. 15, 45.

The publishers would like to thank the following for permission to use material for which they hold the copyright: Hodder & Stoughton Ltd for the extracts from *Teach Yourself World Faiths: Sikhism* by W. Owen Cole on pp. 7, 13, 19, 35, 43; Macmillan Publishers Ltd. for the adapted extract from *An Advanced History of India,* ed. R. C. Majumdar, H. C. Raychaudhuri and Kalikinkar Datta, on p. 25; The Sikh Missionary Society U.K. for the extracts from *The Sikh Symbols* on pp. 9, 23, the extracts from *The Supreme Sacrifice of Guru Tegh Bahadur* on pp. 29, 31 and the extract from *The Sikh Woman* on p. 39; Stanley Thornes (Publishers) Ltd. for the adapted extracts from *World Religions: Sikhism* by Piara Singh Sambhi on pp. 11 and 21 and the adapted extract from *Five Religions in the Twentieth Century* by W. Owen Cole on p. 27.

The publishers have made every effort to trace the copyright holders, but if they have inadvertently overlooked any, they will be pleased to make the necessary arrangements at the first opportunity.

CONTENTS

MAP: WHERE THE MAIN RELIGIONS BEGAN

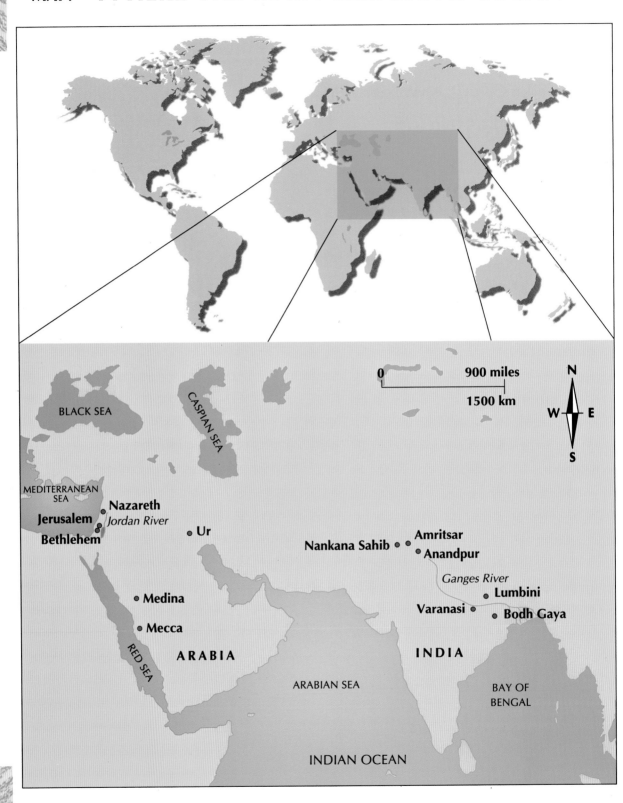

BLACK SEA

CASPIAN SEA

MEDITERRANEAN SEA

Nazareth
Jerusalem
Jordan River
Bethlehem

Ur

Nankana Sahib

Amritsar
Anandpur

Ganges River

Medina

Lumbini

Varanasi
Bodh Gaya

Mecca

RED SEA

ARABIA

INDIA

ARABIAN SEA

BAY OF BENGAL

INDIAN OCEAN

0   900 miles

1500 km

N
W   E
S

TIME CHART: WHEN THE MAIN RELIGIONS BEGAN

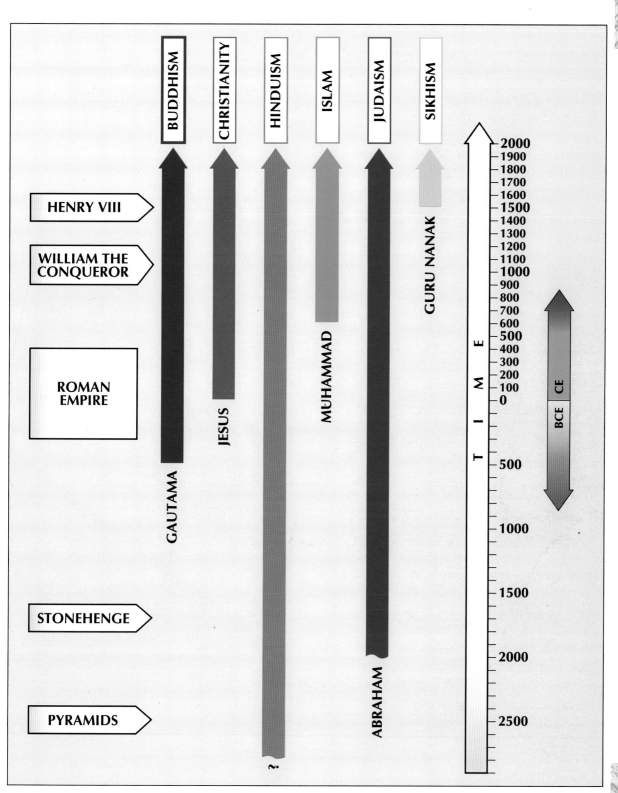

Note about dating systems

In this book dates are not called BC and AD which is the Christian dating system. The letters BCE and CE are used instead. BCE stands for Before the Common Era and CE stands for Common Era. BCE and CE can be used by people of all religions, Christians too. The year numbers are not changed.

INTRODUCING SIKHISM

This section tells you something about who Sikhs are.

Sikhs are followers of the religion of Sikhism. The word Sikh comes from the **Punjabi** language, which is spoken by many Sikhs. It means learner or **disciple**. Sikhism began in India in the sixteenth century, but today there are Sikhs in many countries of the world.

Sikhs follow the teachings of **Gurus**. Guru is a title that is often used in India for religious teachers. Sikhs believe that ten Gurus were especially important. They were spiritual guides who gave human beings God's teachings. These teachings show Sikhs how to live. The first Guru of the Sikhs was a man called Guru Nanak. (See page 16.) The tenth Guru said that there would be no more human Gurus after him. Instead, the Sikhs' teacher would be their holy book. This is why the holy book of the Sikhs is called the **Guru Granth Sahib**. Granth means a large book. Sahib is a title that shows respect.

What do Sikhs believe?

Sikhs believe that there is one God who is almighty and **eternal**. This means that God was never born and will never die. God made the universe and everything in it, and is present everywhere and in everything. Human beings cannot understand God, but God is good and cares about everything in creation. One of Guru Nanak's hymns says, "You are our mother and father, and we are your children." God is a spirit who should be loved, prayed to, and worshiped. Sikhism teaches that God is the greatest Guru, and it is wrong to worship anything except God. Two names that Sikhs often use for God are **Satnam,** which means eternal reality, and **Raheguru,** which means wonderful Lord.

Notice that care has been taken not to use "he" or "she" when referring to God. Sikhs believe that God created male and female, but is neither male nor female. Guru Nanak said, "God is neither a woman nor a man nor a bird," and Sikhs therefore do not describe God as being male or female.

The Sikh symbol.

The symbol of the Sikhs

The symbol often used for Sikhism is made up of three parts. On the outside there are two swords. These are to show that Sikhs should serve God by teaching the truth and by fighting for what is right. Between the swords is a circle that reminds them that God is one, and has no beginning and no end. In the center is a two-edged sword called a **khanda**. This is a symbol of the power of God.

Another symbol, which Sikhs often use, is made up of letters that mean "there is only one God." These are the first words of the Guru Granth Sahib.

This means "There is only one God."

THE MOOL MANTAR

"Mool Mantar" means basic teaching. These words are said to be the first hymn that Guru Nanak spoke, and they sum up Sikh beliefs about God. They are the words that begin the Guru Granth Sahib.

> *There is one supreme eternal reality; the truth; immanent in all things; sustainer of all things; creator of all things; immanent in creation. Without fear and without hatred; not subject to time; beyond birth and death; self-revealing. Known by the Guru's grace.*

NEW WORDS

Disciple A follower of a particular teacher.
Eternal Lasting forever.
Guru A religious teacher (for Sikhs, one of ten religious leaders).
Guru Granth Sahib Sikh holy book.
Khanda Two-edged sword.
Punjabi Language spoken by most Sikhs.
Raheguru The Sikh name for God.
Satnam The Sikh name for God.

THE FIVE K'S

This section tells you about the special things that Sikhs who are full members of the religion wear to show their faith.

Everyone who is a full member of the Sikh religion should wear five symbols to show that they are Sikhs. These symbols are often called the five K's because in the Punjabi language, which many Sikhs speak, their names all begin with the letter *K*. The five K's were introduced by the tenth Guru, Guru Gobind Singh. Each of them reminds Sikhs of something about their religion.

Kesh

Kesh means uncut hair. The Guru said that hair should be allowed to grow naturally. For men, this includes not shaving. At the time of Guru Gobind Singh, some holy men let their hair become tangled and dirty. The Guru said that this was not right. Hair should be allowed to grow, but it should be kept clean and should be combed at least twice a day.

Kangha

The kangha is a small comb. It is worn in the hair and is used to keep the hair fixed in place. For Sikhs, keeping clean and neat is part of their religion. Combing their hair reminds them that their lives should be tidy and organized, too.

Kirpan

The kirpan is a sword. It reminds Sikhs that it is their duty to fight against evil. A kirpan should never be used for attacking people. A kirpan may be up to a three feet (1 m) long, but most Sikhs today carry a short sword about 4 inches (10 cm) long. It is usually kept in a special case fixed to a strap over the person's shoulder.

Kara

The kara is a steel bangle worn on the right wrist. At first, it was probably broader than the one that Sikhs wear today and was intended to protect the arm in battle. Today it is worn as a symbol. The circle reminds Sikhs that God

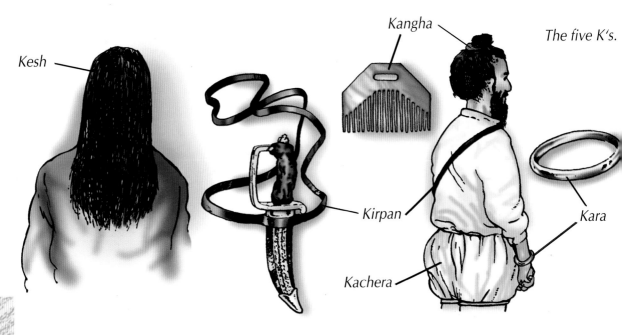

Kesh

Kangha

The five K's.

Kirpan

Kara

Kachera

has no beginning and no end. The steel reminds them of the strength they must have when fighting for what is right.

Kachera

Kachera are short trousers that are worn as underwear. At the time when they were introduced, most people in India wore long, loose clothes. Guru Gobind Singh said that the change in style was a symbol that people were leaving behind old ideas and following better ones. Kachera were also more practical, especially in battle.

The turban

The turban is not one of the five K's, but many male Sikhs and some female Sikhs wear one. It has become one of the symbols of Sikhism. It is a long piece of cloth that is wound around the head so that it covers the head. Turbans help to keep the long hair neat, but they are also worn because they copy what the Sikh Gurus wore.

This Sikh boy is wearing a turban and the five K's.

THE IMPORTANCE OF THE FIVE K'S

This is part of a letter written by Guru Gobind Singh to Sikhs in Afghanistan.

> *The Guru will be your support forever. I am much pleased with you all. You must take the baptism of the sword from five; keep your hair uncut—this is the seal of the Guru. Never be complacent about the pair of shorts and the sword. Always wear on your wrist a steel bracelet, keep your hair neat and clean and comb it twice a day. Always read and recite the hymns of the Guru. Meditate on the name of the wonderful Lord—God alone. Keep the symbols of the faith as the Guru has told you.*

Guru Gobind Singh to the Sikhs of Kabul, June 1699 CE

THE GURDWARA

This section tells you about the Sikh place of worship.

The Sikh place of worship is called the **gurdwara**. This means Guru's door—in other words, a gurdwara is God's house. A gurdwara does not have to be a special building. Especially outside India, gurdwaras may be in ordinary houses or in other buildings. The important thing is not the building. It is the fact that the Guru Granth Sahib, the Sikh holy book, is there.

All gurdwaras have some things in common. There is always a room where the people meet for worship. If the building is large enough, there is also a small room where the Guru Granth Sahib is kept when it is not in the worship room. A kitchen is essential. It is part of Sikh worship that everyone present should be able to share a meal when the service is over. At the entrance to the gurdwara there are separate rooms where men and women can wash their hands and feet, and areas where they can leave their shoes. No one wears shoes in the worship room. Sikhs are expected not to smoke or drink alcohol, so these things are not allowed in a gurdwara.

Outside the gurdwara

Gurdwaras that are specially built may have a dome and decorations on the outside, but these are not essential. The one thing that all gurdwaras can be recognized by is the flag that flies outside. It is yellow, with the Sikh symbol on it, and is called the **Nishan Sahib**. It always flies above the level of the building.

The worship room

The proper name for the worship room is the diwan hall. It is often decorated with tinsel and small lights. There may be pictures of Guru Nanak and the other Gurus on the walls, although some Sikhs do not approve of this because they think people may begin to worship the pictures. The diwan hall usually has a carpet, but there are no seats. All worshipers sit on the floor as a sign that everyone is equal. The most important part of the room is the platform at one end. This is called the **takht**, which means throne. The Guru Granth Sahib is placed upon it on a special stool called a **manji**. The takht is the same sort of throne as a human guru would sit on, and shows that the book is treated with the same respect. In front of the takht is a place where people can leave gifts of food or money.

A gurdwara in a Western city.

A takht.

The langar

Sikh services are always followed by a meal that is called the **langar**. Everyone at the service is welcome at the langar, too. It is an important part of Sikh worship that goes back to the days of Guru Nanak. In India at that time, there were strict rules which said that different groups of people should not eat together. Guru Nanak said that being a Sikh was more important than these rules, and the meal became a symbol of the Sikh belief that all people are equal. The food is cooked and served by both men and women, and is given free to everyone. It is paid for by money that people give at the beginning of the service and by other offerings. The meal is intended to be simple and wholesome, and always consists of dishes that would be eaten in the Punjab, no matter where in the world the gurdwara is. The food is vegetarian, so that people who do not eat meat can still take part.

NEW WORDS

Gurdwara Sikh place of worship.
Langar A free meal that ends Sikh services.
Manji Stool the Guru Granth Sahib is placed on.
Nishan Sahib Sikh flag.
Takht "Throne" for Guru Granth Sahib.

THE IMPORTANCE OF WORSHIP

These words come from the writings of the fourth Guru. They show how important worship is for Sikhs.

He who calls himself a disciple of the great Sat Guru (God) should rise early in the morning and meditate on God's name. He should rise early, take a bath and make an effort to wash himself in the Pool of Nectar (God). By repeating God's name according to the Guru's instructions, all evil deeds and mistakes will be washed away. Afterwards, at sunrise he should sing the hymns of praise composed by the Guru; he should remember the name (of God) while performing daily chores. The person who repeats the name with every breath is a dear disciple of the Guru.

Adi Granth 305–6 Guru Ram Das

WORSHIP IN THE GURDWARA

This section tells you about how Sikhs worship in the gurdwara.

Sikhs do not have a particular day of worship. Many gurdwaras are open from dawn to sunset every day for people to come in to pray, with services in the morning and evening. In the United States, the main services are usually held on a Sunday, because it is a convenient day for many people. The most important room in a gurdwara is the worship room where Sikhs meet together in the same place as the Guru Granth Sahib. They say that this is like being in front of God.

Any Sikh who is respected by the others may lead the worship in a gurdwara. There is usually one person in each gurdwara whose job is to read from the Guru Granth Sahib and to lead the prayers. This person is called the **granthi**. He or she sits behind the Guru Granth Sahib, facing the rest of the people. Sometimes the granthi waves a **chauri** over the Guru Granth Sahib. This is a special fan made of hair or feathers. It is the same kind of fan that was held over kings in India, and is waved over the Guru Granth Sahib to show the same respect.

Before they go into the worship room, everyone takes off their shoes. They may wash their

A Sikh service.

hands and feet, or may have had a bath at home before coming to the gurdwara. Any man who is not wearing a turban covers his head. These things are all to show respect for the Guru Granth Sahib. When they go into the room, the people go to the front and bow or kneel in front of the Guru Granth Sahib. They leave offerings of food or money. As they go to sit down, they are careful never to turn their backs on the Guru Granth Sahib, because this would show a lack of respect. The people sit on the floor to show that everyone is equal, and that the Guru Granth Sahib is the most important thing in the room. It is usual for men and women to sit on opposite sides of the room.

Worship

Services in a gurdwara are usually held in Punjabi, the language spoken by most Sikhs. They may last up to five hours, but they are very relaxed, and people are not expected to stay for the whole time. They may arrive after the beginning or leave before the end.

Musicians are very important in Sikh services.

The Ardas.

The aim of Sikh worship is to give praise to God. Most worship consists of reading and singing of hymns from the Guru Granth Sahib and from other books like the writings of the Gurus. The singing of the hymns is called **kirtan** and is very important. It is done by musicians called **ragis**, and the people do not always join in the singing. There are talks that help to explain the **Scriptures**, or talks about things that affect Sikhs in their lives.

The Ardas

All services end with the **Ardas**, a special prayer that lasts about fifteen minutes. Everyone stands, with one person in front of the rest, facing the Guru Granth Sahib. This person leads the prayer that reminds everyone to remember God and the ten Gurus, and to pass on the teachings of the Guru Granth Sahib. Prayers are said for Sikhs and all people everywhere, and there may be special prayers for people who are ill or who need prayers for some other reason.

While the Ardas is being said, the **Karah parshad** is stirred with a kirpan. Karah parshad is a special dessert or food that is made of equal quantities of flour, sugar and ghee (specially prepared butter) and mixed in an iron bowl. It is given to everyone who has attended the service, as a symbol that everyone is equal. At the end of the service, everyone shares the special meal called the langar.

NEW WORDS

Ardas Prayer that ends service.
Chauri Special fan.
Granthi Person who leads worship.
Karah parshad Special food given out at the end of Sikh services.
Kirtan Singing of hymns from the Guru Granth Sahib.
Ragi Sikh musician.
Scriptures Holy books.

THE ANAND SAHIB

These words from the Anand Sahib are part of the prayers that come at the end of every service in the gurdwara. They were written by the third Guru.

Listen to my joy, my fortunate friends. All my desires have been fulfilled. I have reached God, the supreme spirit, and all my sorrows have vanished. Sorrow, affliction, and suffering have been relieved through hearing the true word. Saints and holy people are glad on hearing it from the perfect Guru. Pure are the hearers; starless the speakers. The true Guru will fill their hearts. Nanak says, heavenly trumpets sound for those who bow at the Guru's feet.

Anand Sahib v40 Guru Amar Das

THE GURU GRANTH SAHIB

This section tells you about the Sikh holy books.

The Guru Granth Sahib

The most important of the Sikh holy books is the Guru Granth Sahib. It was begun by the first Guru, Guru Nanak. He composed hundreds of hymns praising God, and 974 of them are in the Guru Granth Sahib. In 1604 CE the fifth Guru, Guru Arjan, had an official collection of hymns put together. This contained the hymns of Guru Nanak and hymns written by the other Gurus. It also contained hymns written by **Hindu** and **Muslim** holy men. The hymns praise God and say what God is like. They also include advice about the right way to live. This book is called the *Adi Granth*, which means original book. Guru Arjan had a special building erected where it could be kept. The original Adi Granth still exists today, and Sikhism is the only religion in the world that still has the first copy of its holy book.

Removing the covers from the Guru Granth Sahib.

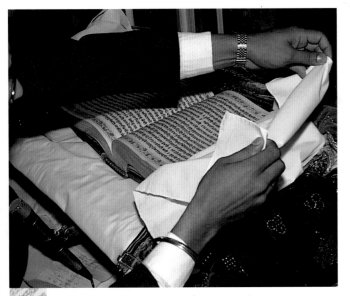

In 1706 CE, the tenth Guru added hymns that had been written by his father, the ninth Guru. This completed the Guru Granth Sahib and, since that date, nothing has been added or taken away from it. For nearly 200 years, copies of it were written out by hand, very carefully so that no mistakes were made. In 1852, the first copy was printed. Sikhs decided that every copy should be exactly the same, and so today every copy of the Guru Granth Sahib has the same number of pages—1430—and particular hymns are always to be found on the same page.

Some Sikhs have their own copy of the Guru Granth Sahib at home. They believe that, because it is so important, it should not be placed on a shelf like other books, but should have a room of its own. This room then becomes a gurdwara, because the Guru Granth Sahib is there. For many Sikhs, of course, this is not possible, so instead, most have a smaller book called a **gutka**. This contains the most important hymns and the daily prayers. A gutka, too, is treated with great respect, and is kept wrapped in a cloth when it is not being used. Before reading from it, Sikhs will wash their hands.

The Guru Granth Sahib is used in all Sikh worship, and it takes the most important place in the gurdwara. Weddings are held in front of it, and it is used to help in the naming of babies. When it is open it is kept on the takht, resting on a cloth and three cushions. There is always someone sitting behind it, and it is never left unattended. When it is closed it is carefully covered with special cloths. A Guru Granth Sahib is put away at night in a special ceremony called **Sukhasan**. The reverse ceremony in a morning is called **Parkash karna**. Carrying the Guru Granth Sahib is a great honor. It is always held above the person's head. Sikhs

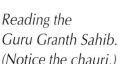

*Reading the
Guru Granth Sahib.
(Notice the chauri.)*

respect the Guru Granth Sahib in this way
because they believe it is the word of God.

Other holy books

No other holy book is as important for Sikhs as
the Guru Granth Sahib, but there are other
books that contain important Sikh writings.
The Dasam Granth ("Book of the tenth Guru")
contains hymns that were written by Guru
Gobind Singh, some of which are used in Sikh
worship. There are also books that help to
explain parts of the Guru Granth Sahib. These
are used when hymns are being explained as
part of the service in a gurdwara.

NEW WORDS

Gutka Book containing the most
important Sikh hymns.
Hindu Follower of the religion of
Hinduism.
Muslim Follower of the religion of
Islam.
Parkash karna Ceremony of returning
the Guru Granth Sahib to the takht.
Sukhasan Ceremony of laying the Guru
Granth Sahib to rest.

A HYMN PRAISING GOD

This is part of the hymn that is sung
as the Guru Granth Sahib is taken
from the place where it has been
overnight and is prepared to be
read from.

> When I come into your presence
> I feel love. My hopes are fulfilled
> by your grace. Hear my request
> for the gift of being able to
> meditate on you and be your
> disciple. God, my true friend,
> listen to my prayer, which is
> that you should remain in my
> heart forever. May I never for-
> get you, the treasure house of
> my virtue.

Guru Granth Sahib 741

SIKH GURUS 1

This section tells you about the life of the first Sikh Guru.

The life of Guru Nanak

The first Guru of Sikhism was called Nanak. He was born in 1469 CE in a village in northern India called Talwindi. Today the town is called Nankana Sahib, in honor of the Guru. There are many stories about Nanak's birth and childhood that show that he was an unusual child, and he became a very religious young man.

Nanak's parents were Hindus, and Nanak was brought up to be a Hindu, too. When he grew up, he began work in a government office. Today, we would say that he was an accountant. The people in the office were Muslims, followers of the religion of Islam. Muslims have beliefs that are very different from the beliefs of Hindus. Nanak obviously enjoyed talking to people about their beliefs, and he learned a lot about the two religions. Nanak married when he was nineteen, and he and his wife had two sons. It seemed that he had everything in life that he could want.

One morning when he was about 30 years old, Nanak went to bathe in the river as usual. Then he disappeared. People searched for him for three days. When they could find no trace of him, it was thought that he must have drowned. Then he returned. The first thing he said was, "There is neither Hindu nor Muslim." This was very puzzling, but he told the people that while he was away he had been taken to see God. He had had a vision in which he had learned that just following a religion did not make people any different. Doing what the religion says—going on **pilgrimages** or making offerings—does not make a person religious. It is the way they live that really matters, and this comes from knowing God. Nanak said that he had been told by God to spend the rest of his life teaching people. A respected teacher of religion in India is called a guru, so, from this time on, Nanak was called Guru Nanak. He called himself Nanak Das, which means Nanak, the slave of God.

The four journeys of Guru Nanak.

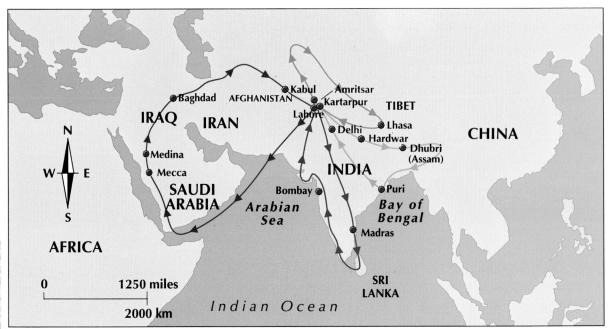

Guru Nanak.

One man who came to join the group was called Lehna. He became one of Guru Nanak's closest followers. Just before he died, in 1539, Guru Nanak said that Lehna was to be the next Guru. He gave him a new name, Angad, which means "part of me." Guru Angad was to carry on the work that Guru Nanak had begun.

NEW WORDS

Meditate Think deeply, especially about religion.
Pilgrimage Journey made for religious reasons.

For the next 20 years, Guru Nanak traveled. He went to Varanasi, the holy city of Hindus, and to many other places in India. He went to Arabia and the Muslim holy city of Mecca, and to the countries that today are called Iraq, Tibet, and Sri Lanka. Wherever he went, he told people that the way to find God was in the way they lived and what they believed.

At last, Guru Nanak settled in a village called Kartarpur in northern India. A group of people who wanted to follow his teachings came to live nearby. They became the first Sikhs. *Sikh* comes from a word that means "someone who learns," and the people came to learn from the Guru. They met together to **meditate** in the morning and evening, listened to Guru Nanak preach, and joined in singing the hymns that the Guru had written. An important part of their life in Kartarpur was that they often ate together. Free food was given to everyone, no matter what religion or social group they came from. In India at that time it was unheard of for people to eat like this, but Guru Nanak said that it was very important.

HOW GURU NANAK WAS CALLED BY GOD

This is how Guru Nanak described how God told him to become a preacher:

> I was a minstrel out of work.
>
> I became attached to divine service.
>
> The Almighty one commissioned me,
>
> "Night and day sing my praise."
>
> The master summoned the minstrel
>
> To the high court, and robed me with the clothes of honor,
>
> To sing God's praises.

Adi Granth 150

SIKH GURUS II

This section tells you about the three Gurus who followed Guru Nanak.

After Guru Nanak there were nine other Gurus. Each one was chosen by the one before, and each one continued Guru Nanak's teaching. Sikhs believe that all the Gurus shared Guru Nanak's spirit. They say that the Gurus were like candles that have been lighted from each other. All of the Gurus worked to develop the new faith. Some had to guide Sikhs through times of **persecution**, when they were punished and even killed for what they believed.

Guru Angad (1539–1552)

The second Guru was Guru Angad. He was chosen by Guru Nanak himself. There is a Sikh story that he was chosen after Guru Nanak had planned a test to see who should be the next Guru. He dropped a cup into a muddy ditch and asked his two sons to get it for him. They both refused because they thought it was not right for a Guru's son to do a servant's job. Angad jumped down into the ditch and fetched the cup without even being asked.

Guru Angad is remembered as being the Guru who worked out **gurmukhi**—the alphabet that all the Sikh Scriptures are written in. At the time of Guru Nanak, there was no agreed written form of Punjabi, the language that he spoke. People in those days were able to remember things without writing them down, but Guru Angad made a collection of Guru Nanak's hymns, and obviously felt that it was important for them to be written down. Gurmukhi means "from the mouth of the Guru." Guru Angad also wrote some hymns himself. The name of Guru Nanak is mentioned in the last line of all of them. This is a way of showing that he was carrying on the teachings of Guru Nanak.

Guru Angad began providing education for young people and encouraged them to learn gurmukhi. This was a way of helping to make sure that Sikhism continued. He also began building places where Sikhs could worship—gurdwaras.

Guru Amar Das (1552–1574)

Guru Angad was only 48 years old when he died, and he chose a distant relative to be the next Guru. This man was Guru Amar Das, who continued the work of spreading the message of Sikhism. He stressed the importance of women preachers, and he was the first Guru to choose men and women to go out and preach to other people about the new faith. He began the custom of having all Sikhs who could get there meet twice a year at his hometown of Goindwal. These meetings were at festival times. This meant that he could meet them all himself, and it was also important in keeping the new religion separate. Guru Amar Das also

The Guru Granth Sahib is written in gurmukhi.

Amritsar, a city where building was started by Guru Ram Das.

continued Guru Nanak's teaching about how important it was that everyone be able to eat together. On one occasion, the Emperor came to see him, and the Guru insisted that he too should sit with everyone else and share the meal. The langar that all gurdwaras serve continues this teaching.

Guru Ram Das (1574–1581)

Guru Ram Das was Guru Amar Das' son-in-law. He is remembered especially for writing the hymns that Sikhs use at weddings and for beginning the buildings that became the Sikh city of Amritsar, in the Punjab.

NEW WORDS

Gurmukhi Written form of the Punjabi language.
Persecution The act of treating someone badly because of their religion.

A HYMN OF GURU AMAR DAS

This is part of a hymn called the Anand, which was composed by the third Guru. It is used by Sikhs every-day when they meditate, and it is also used in the amrit ceremony. (See page 23).

> *O my mind, concentrate on God, stick to God!*
>
> *Your sufferings will vanish.*
>
> *If God accepts you, you will succeed.*
>
> *God is almighty and can do anything for you, so why forget God?*
>
> *O my mind, keep fixed on God always.*

Adi Granth 917

19

SIKH GURUS III

This section tells you about the later Gurus.

Guru Arjan (1581–1606)

Guru Arjan was the first Guru who was born a Sikh. He took over from his father, Guru Ram Das. Guru Arjan continued the building at Amritsar that his father had begun and built a beautiful gurdwara in the middle of an artificial lake. This gurdwara is now the Golden Temple, the most important building in the Sikh religion. Guru Arjan put together the Adi Granth (see page 14) and placed it in this building.

At this time, the Sikhs enjoyed good relations with the rulers of the country. However, in 1605 CE the Emperor of India died, and the new Emperor accused Guru Arjan of helping a rival for the throne. He was arrested and tortured to death in 1606. This led to a change in the way Sikhs thought about themselves.

Guru Har Gobind (1606–1644)

Guru Har Gobind became Guru after his father had been killed. He realized that the Sikhs needed to form an army if they were going to survive. They had to be able to defend themselves with force if it became necessary. He was Guru for nearly 40 years, and in that time he lived like a soldier and worked hard to make sure that many Sikhs became excellent fighters. When he died in 1644, his grandson became the next Guru.

Guru Har Rai (1644–1661)

Guru Har Rai worked to make the religion of Sikhism stronger. During his time, Sikhism spread more widely in northern India. He tried to make peace in the wars between the Sikhs and Muslims. Before he died, he chose his son to be the next Guru.

Guru Har Krishan (1661–1664)

Guru Har Krishan was only five years old when he became Guru, and he died when he was only eight. He is mainly remembered for the fact that he died of smallpox that he caught while he was caring for people who were suffering from the disease.

Guru Tegh Bahadur (1664–1675)

Guru Tegh Bahadur was the son of Guru Har Gobind. While he was Guru, the Sikhs were being persecuted again. Guru Tegh Bahadur was beheaded in 1675, because he refused to change his religion. (This story is told in more detail on page 30.) Sikhs remember him with pride because he was ready to give up his life, but not his faith.

Guru Gobind Singh (1675–1708)

Guru Gobind Singh became the tenth Guru when he was only nine years old. He is remembered as being the most important Guru after Guru Nanak. He began the **Khalsa** (see page 22), the brotherhood of Sikhs who are full members of the religion. The special clothes that Sikhs wear, the five K's, date from this time. Just before he died, Guru Gobind Singh said that he was not going to choose a new human Guru, as the other Gurus had done. He said that in the future the Guru would be the Sikh holy book. This contained the teachings of the Gurus, and it would be the Sikhs' only teacher. Since that time, it has been called the Guru Granth Sahib.

NEW WORD

Khalsa Sikhs who have taken part in the amrit ceremony.

Guru Gobind Singh.

A PRAYER OF GURU ARJAN

This prayer is by the fifth Guru. It is often sung in the gurdwara.

O God, I lean on you for you are always with me.

Be merciful, O my Lord, that I contemplate ever your name filled with love.

I have no other support.

I accept whatever you do or cause to be done.

You are my honor. Your nearness is my deliverance, your virtuous words my riches.

O, God, Nanak seeks the refuge of your feet for this is what he has learned from holy men.

Adi Granth 677

THE KHALSA

This section tells you about the beginning of the Khalsa.

At the time of the tenth Guru, Guru Gobind Singh, the Sikhs were being persecuted and killed for what they believed. The Guru decided that they needed to form a fighting force that could defend the faith.

In 1699, Guru Gobind Singh called all the Sikhs to a meeting at Anandpur, in northern India. This took place at the spring festival of Baisakhi. When all the Sikhs were together, he told them that they needed to be strong to fight the people who were persecuting them. He asked if any of the Sikhs were willing to die for what they believed. No one answered. He repeated the question. Still no one answered. He asked a third time. At last, one man came forward. The Guru took him into his tent. There was a thud, and the Guru returned with a blood-stained sword. He asked the question again. Another man came forward, saying he was prepared to die, too. The same thing happened. Three more men were taken away, one by one. The people were terrified, thinking that the Guru had killed them all.

After the fifth time, the Guru went away. When he returned, all five men were with him! They were dressed in yellow robes like his own. Guru Gobind Singh told the people that because the men had been prepared to die for what they believed, they should be called the **panj piare** —the beloved ones. They would be the first members of a new group. It would be called the *Khalsa*, which means "the pure ones." Sikhs could only belong to this group if they were without fear, and ready to die for their faith.

When the people understood what the Guru wanted, many more men and women came forward to become members of the Khalsa. The Guru said that being part of the Khalsa was

These men are dressed to represent the panj piare.

more important than anything else. So to show that they were all equal, they had to do two things. One was to drink **amrit** from the same bowl. (In those days, people of different backgrounds were not allowed to eat or drink together.) Amrit is a special mixture of sugar and water that is stirred with a khanda, the two-edged sword. The second thing was to use the same name. This was a symbol that they were one family in the faith. Men were to take the name "Singh," which means lion. Women were to take the name "Kaur," which means princess. Since that time, all Sikhs have used these names as part of their own names.

Not all Sikhs today are members of the Khalsa. Some feel that they cannot keep the rules for living of the group, and some do not feel that membership is important for them. Sikhs who do become members must be old enough to understand what it involves. Many do not join until they are middle-aged. When a Sikh joins the Khalsa, there is a special ceremony called the **amrit ceremony**.

The amrit ceremony

The amrit ceremony must take place in front of the Guru Granth Sahib. But it cannot take place in the worship room, which is open to anyone. Only Sikhs who have taken amrit may be present, except for those who wish to join. Everyone wears the five K's, and five Sikhs represent the panj piare. A sixth reads from the Guru Granth Sahib. One of the five beloved ones repeats the duties that members of the Khalsa must keep, and there are prayers and readings from the Guru Granth Sahib. Those who wish to join kneel in a special position resting on their right knee with the left one raised. This is a symbol that they are ready to defend their faith. Each person drinks some of the amrit, and it is sprinkled into their eyes, hair, and hands. After more prayers, the ceremony ends with everyone eating Karah parshad. When they have taken part in this ceremony, Sikhs are expected to keep all the rules and duties of their religion.

Washing the feet is part of the preparations for the amrit ceremony.

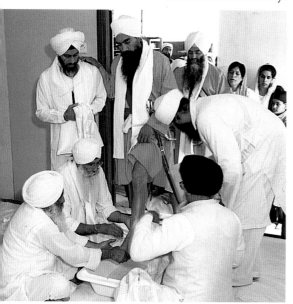

NEW WORDS

Amrit Special mixture of sugar and water.
Amrit ceremony Ceremony in which people become members of the Khalsa.
Panj piare Beloved ones—first members of the Khalsa.

THE KHALSA

This passage comes from a Sikh code of conduct. Although it only uses "he," the Khalsa is open to both men and women.

> He is of the Khalsa, who is absorbed in God's name.
> He is of the Khalsa, who is devoted to the Guru.
> He is of the Khalsa, who speaks evil of no one.
> He is of the Khalsa, who conquers evil passions.
> He is of the Khalsa, who stands by the oppressed.
> He is of the Khalsa, who does not covet another's wife or wealth.
> He is of the Khalsa, who rides a fiery steed.
> He is of the Khalsa, who fights in the vanguard.
> He is of the Khalsa, who is as hard as steel.
> He is of the Khalsa, who dies for his faith.

Sikh Rahit Nama

SIKH HISTORY

This section tells you something about the history of Sikhism.

Sikhism was begun by Guru Nanak in the sixteenth century. He lived in the part of northern India that is called the Punjab, but he traveled all over India and to many other countries, talking to people about their religion. He became sure that God had a special message for him to pass on to other people. The message was that what religion you follow is not the most important thing. It is knowing God—what you believe and how you live your life—that is really important.

For 200 years after Guru Nanak's death, Sikhs were led by a succession of nine other Gurus. While they were leaders, many changes were made as the new religion developed. Some of the most important changes were made by the tenth Guru, Guru Gobind Singh. He began the Khalsa, which really made Sikhism a separate religion, able to fight for its survival.

At the time of Guru Gobind Singh, Sikhs were being persecuted again for their beliefs. The rulers of the country tried to impose their own religion, and anyone who did not obey was punished. After Guru Gobind Singh's death, groups of Sikhs joined together to try to fight for their faith and for their own country. This meant that the persecution got worse, and for the next 100 years anyone who was known to be a Sikh was in danger of being killed. Many gurdwaras either closed or were cared for by Hindus, and many Sikhs began following their religion in secret and did not wear the five K's or a turban.

Things began to improve for them when a young soldier called Ranjit Singh became a leader in the army. Battles were won, and he became the ruler of an empire that included the Punjab and much of northern India. He ruled for 40 years, and many Sikhs think of this as being a golden age for Sikhs. However, other Sikhs point out that although he was a good ruler in many ways, Ranjit Singh did not

The Punjab.

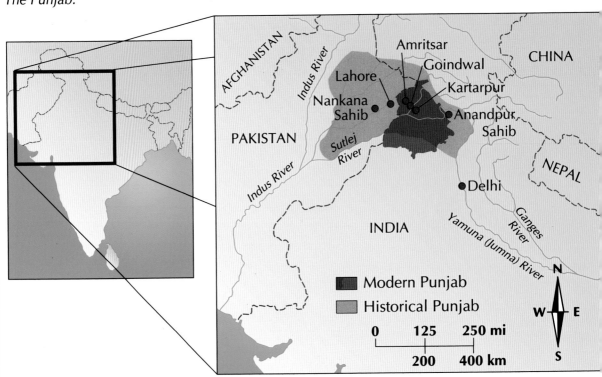

Ranjit Singh.

Pakistan and India cut through the middle of the Punjab. Many Sikhs were bitterly disappointed. They had hoped that Sikhs would be given their own country. There were riots when Sikhs were forced to leave Pakistan, and thousands of people were killed. Many Sikhs would still like to create an independent Sikh country, which they would call Khalistan. In recent years, this has been the reason for much of the fighting which has taken place in India and the Punjab.

always follow the teachings of Sikhism himself. (For example, he had several Hindu wives.) Sikhs had freedom from persecution, but little was done to return to the teachings of the Gurus.

After the death of Ranjit Singh, the army became less powerful, and in 1849 the British took control of the Punjab as they increased their rule over India. There were treaties with Sikh leaders and more freedom from persecution. Sikh leaders began to try to return to the "pure" Sikhism that had been taught by the Gurus. There were still many struggles to keep Sikhism a separate religion, but in 1909 Sikhs in India won the right to hold their own marriage services rather than have weddings conducted by Hindu priests. This was a major victory, and it was followed by Acts of Parliament that returned control of gurdwaras to Sikhs.

Khalistan

When the British left India in 1947, the new country of Pakistan was created. It was to be a country for Muslims. The border between

RANJIT SINGH

This is how a history of India describes Ranjit Singh.

Ranjit Singh is one of the most important personalities in the history of modern India. Though his physical appearance was not particularly handsome, and an attack of smallpox meant that he was blind in the left eye, he had delightful manners and inspiring features. He was a religious man himself, and he respected religion in others. He said that every success was due to the favor of God, and he styled himself and his people the Khalsa, or "Commonwealth of Gobind."

An Advanced History of India (adapted)

HOLY PLACES

This section tells you about the places that are most important for Sikhs.

Some religions expect their followers to go on pilgrimages—journeys to places that are particularly important for that religion. The Gurus were quite clear in their teaching about pilgrimage. They said that it is not necessary because God is equally present everywhere. However, there are many places that Sikhs like to visit, usually because they are connected with events in Sikh history.

Amritsar

The most important building in the Sikh religion is the Golden Temple at Amritsar, in the Punjab. The temple is built on a platform 215 square feet (20 m²), in the middle of an artificial lake. It was built with four entrances, as a symbol that people from all over the world are welcome there. In the nineteenth century, the Sikh ruler Ranjit Singh had the temple rebuilt in marble. The top half was then covered with gold leaf, and it was after this that it became known as the "Golden Temple." Its proper name is Harminder Sahib, which means temple of God. The walls of the Golden Temple have verses from the Guru Granth Sahib carved on them, and the Temple contains very old handwritten copies of the Guru Granth Sahib. Readings from it begin at dawn, and the singing of hymns goes on until late at night everyday in the Temple. There is a special procession every morning and night when the Guru Granth Sahib is carried to and from the worship room to the room where it spends the night. To take part in the procession is a great honor for Sikhs. Facing the Golden Temple opposite the main gateway is a building called the Akal Takht. This was built by the sixth Guru. Important meetings of Sikhs from all over the world are held there.

The Golden Temple at Amritsar.

This gurdwara is at Anandpur.

Nankana Sahib

Most important places for Sikhs are connected with the Gurus, and Nankana Sahib is the town where Guru Nanak grew up. It is now in Pakistan. It used to be called Talwindi, but its name was changed to honor the Guru. There are several gurdwaras there that were built to remind people of events in his life.

Anandpur

Anandpur is a town in a valley near the Himalayan mountains. It was there that the tenth Guru began the Khalsa. It is also the place where the head of Guru Tegh Bahadur was **cremated** after he had been beheaded for refusing to give up his faith.

Hazur Sahib

Hazur Sahib is a gurdwara in the town of Nander in southern India. It marks the place where Guru Gobind Singh died. There is a museum in the gurdwara where some of the Guru's clothes are kept. There is also a horse that is descended from the one that the Guru used to ride. This horse is used in the processions in the town that celebrate events in the lives of the Gurus.

NEW WORD

Cremate Burn a body after death.

THE SIKH ATTITUDE TO PILGRIMAGE

Sikhs may visit holy places, but they are taught not to go on pilgrimages. This quotation shows that the Gurus believed going on pilgrimages was much less important than what people actually believed.

> If a man goes to bathe at a place of pilgrimage, and he has the mind of a crook and the body of a thief, of course his outside will be washed by the bathing, but his inside will be twice as unclean. He will be like a gourd which is clean on the outside but full of poison on the inside. The saints are pure without such bathing. The thief remains a thief even if he bathes at places of pilgrimage.

Adi Granth 789

FESTIVALS I

This section tells you about festivals celebrating the Gurus' birthdays.

Gurpurbs

Sikhs do not attach a lot of importance to the actual date of festivals, and the celebrations are often held on the weekend that follows if this is more convenient.

Some of the most important Sikh festivals are those which celebrate the birth or death of one of the Gurus. They are called **gurpurbs**, which means a holy day in honor of the Guru. The most important part of a gurpurb is a reading of the Guru Granth Sahib from beginning to end without stopping. This is called an **Akhand Path**.

Akhand Path

An Akhand Path takes about 48 hours, and is timed so that it ends early in a morning. Where it is being read before a gurpurb, it is arranged so that it ends on the morning of the festival. The reading is done by any members of the local Sikh community who can read gurmukhi clearly and accurately. They take turns, reading for no more than two hours at a time. There is always a substitute in case someone is ill, and the readers make sure that no break occurs, with a new reader taking his or her place behind the Guru Granth Sahib as the previous reader comes to the end of their section. The readers must bathe before going to the gurdwara, and immediately before beginning to read they wash their hands, so that they are clean to touch the pages of the Guru Granth Sahib. While the Akhand Path is taking place, Sikhs make a special effort to go to the gurdwara, to listen and meditate. They try very hard to be there for the special ceremony that ends the reading. Langar is served throughout the Akhand Path, so a list of rotating volunteers for cooking, serving, and washing is needed.

Reading the Guru Granth Sahib all the way through is an important part of a gurpurb.

These two boys are taking part in a procession remembering Guru Gobind Singh.

eastern India, which is where the Guru was born. There are also special games and sports competitions to celebrate the festival.

NEW WORDS

Akhand Path Nonstop reading of the Guru Granth Sahib.
Gurpurb Festival in honor of a Guru.

The birthday of Guru Nanak

Guru Nanak was born in 1469 CE, and Sikhs celebrate his birthday in November every year. This is the most important gurpurb, and is celebrated by Sikhs all over the world. The celebrations usually last for three days. In towns or cities where there are large numbers of Sikhs, there are processions through the streets. A procession is led by five people who represent the panj piare, the five men who were the first to join the Khalsa. Like the panj piare, they wear yellow robes, usually with a wide blue belt, and yellow turbans. Immediately behind them is a float that is often beautifully decorated and carries the Guru Granth Sahib. The people in the procession follow, singing hymns that were written by Guru Nanak. Guru Nanak said that it was important for people to be able to eat and drink together, so people watching the procession are often given sweets or fruit and nonalcoholic drinks.

The birthday of Guru Gobind Singh

Guru Gobind Singh was the tenth Guru, and he was born in 1666 CE. His birthday is celebrated in December, and is the second most important gurpurb. Like the other gurpurbs, it is celebrated with processions. One of the most important is in the town of Patna in north-

A PRAYER OF GURU GOBIND SINGH

This was the favorite prayer of Guru Gobind Singh. It is often used by Sikhs today and is sometimes called the "Sikh anthem."

O Lord, grant me the wish that I may never flinch from performing righteous deeds. That I may never be afraid of the enemy, and I may have supreme confidence to win.

Let one directive guide my mind exclusively, that I may ever be singing your praises.

And when the time comes, I should die fighting heroically on the battlefield.

FESTIVALS II

This section tells you about gurpurbs that are held to remember the deaths of two Gurus.

The death of Guru Arjan

Guru Arjan was the fifth Guru. His death is important because Sikhs think of him as the first Sikh **martyr**. A martyr is someone who dies for what they believe. Guru Arjan and the Sikhs became involved accidentally in a quarrel between the ruler of the country and a rival for the throne. The ruler ordered that Guru Arjan be killed, and he was tortured to death.

Like other gurpurbs, Guru Arjan's death is remembered with processions. He was killed in the summer, when it is very hot in India, and part of his torture was that he was not allowed anything to drink. To remind people of his suffering, and as a sign of respect, people watching the processions are given nonalcoholic drinks.

The death of Guru Tegh Bahadur

Guru Tegh Bahadur was the ninth Guru. He was also a martyr. Sikhs are particularly proud of him because he gave his life on behalf of Hindus. At that time the rulers of that part of India were persecuting Sikhs and Hindus. The leaders of the Hindus came to Guru Tegh Bahadur for advice because they knew he was a holy man. He agreed to speak to the Emperor on behalf of Hindus, and he encouraged both Sikhs and Hindus to stick to their faith. The Guru was arrested and taken to the city of Delhi. He was offered all kinds of rewards if he would change his religion, but he would not accept any of them. Then he was forced to watch while three of his followers were tortured to death. Even this did not make Guru Tegh Bahadur change his mind. He still said that it was important that everyone be allowed to worship in the way they wanted. Then the rulers realized that they would not succeed in making Guru Tegh Bahadur change his religion.

This procession celebrates the martyrdom of Guru Tegh Bahadur.

They ordered that he should be killed. His head was cut off.

Sikhs believe that the Guru's death shows an important lesson. He could have saved his own life by changing his religion, but he was acting on behalf of Hindus as well as Sikhs. If he had changed his mind, the persecution would have become worse, and they would have had to give up what they believed, too. He died so that people of a different religion could have freedom to worship as they wished. Sikhs say that this shows how brave he was. To die because you refuse to give up your own beliefs is very brave. To die to save someone else's beliefs is even braver.

The main gurpurb to remember Guru Tegh Bahadur's death is held in Delhi, then capital of India, because this is where he was killed. There are processions through the streets that end at a very beautiful gurdwara which is built over the place where he was beheaded. Then the people go to the gurdwara to worship.

NEW WORD

Martyr Person who is killed for their beliefs.

THE MARTYRDOM OF GURU TEGH BAHADUR

This is part of a poem written by the tenth Guru that describes the martyrdom.

> To uphold righteousness, so supreme an act did he perform;
>
> He gave his head, but did not utter a word of sorrow.
>
> For the sake of righteousness he did this great heroic deed;
>
> He laid down his life but not the principles...
>
> No one has ever done such a unique deed as did Guru Tegh Bahadur.
>
> On the ascent of Guru Tegh Bahadur, the whole world went into mourning.
>
> Alas! Alas! rose the wailing cries from the earth;
>
> While the shouts of Glory! Glory! resounded the heavens.

Guru Gobind Singh

This gurdwara is built where Guru Tegh Bahadur was killed.

FESTIVALS III

This section tells you about festivals called **melas**.

Sikhs celebrate two kinds of festivals. Gurpurbs remember the birth or death of one of the Gurus. The other kind of festival is a called a mela, which means fair. Melas are often similar to Hindu festivals, but Sikhs celebrate them in their own way.

Baisakhi

Baisakhi is the name of the first month of the year in the Sikh calendar. The festival of Baisakhi is held at the beginning of the month, and so it includes the Sikh new year. In the Western calendar, Baisakhi falls on April 13 or 14. It is celebrated by Sikhs all over the world.

The first Baisakhi took place in 1699 CE, and was the occasion when Guru Gobind Singh began the Khalsa. (See page 22.) The fact that

The Nishan Sahib, the Sikh flag, is replaced at Baisakhi.

Baisakhi is the "birthday" of the Khalsa means that today it is often a popular time for holding the amrit ceremony. That special ceremony is held for people who wish to become full members of the Sikh religion.

At Baisakhi, there are celebrations at the gurdwara all day. The service begins soon after dawn and lasts all morning. People come and go, staying for as long as they can. The langar, the meal that is part of Sikh worship, is often served all day. There are readings from the Guru Granth Sahib, and poems that remind people of the first Baisakhi and how important the day is. Like the gurpurbs, there are processions with the Guru Granth Sahib being carried on a float or other open vehicle, and people singing religious songs. In many places in India there are fairs to celebrate Baisakhi. In the town of Amritsar, there is a famous market which is held every year, where farmers buy and sell all kinds of animals.

Hola Mohalla

Many other melas take place in particular towns or areas. The festival of Hola Mohalla is celebrated particularly in the town of Anandpur in India. This is the town where in 1680 CE the sixth Guru arranged a festival that took place at the same time as an important Hindu festival. This was a way of making people choose whether they were Sikhs or Hindus, because they could not celebrate both festivals. Today, there are sports events and music and poetry competitions, to remind Sikhs of the festival that the Guru began.

NEW WORD

Mela A fair—Sikh festival.

Lighting candles for Divali.

An important part of Baisakhi is the changing of the coverings on the Nishan Sahib—the flag that flies outside every gurdwara. It is taken down, and the flagpole and flag are washed. A new flag may be used, and the yellow covers that are wrapped around the flagpole and the flag are always replaced.

Divali

Divali means festival of lights. It takes place in November or early December. Its name comes from small clay lamps called *divas*. Sikhs remember it as the time when the sixth Guru was released from prison, and the people of Amritsar lit lamps in every house to welcome him home. Ever since this time, lights have been an important part of Sikh celebrations at Divali, and there are often bonfires and fireworks displays.

THE RELEASE OF GURU HAR GOBIND

Sikhs remember this story at Divali.

Guru Har Gobind had been put in prison by the Emperor Jehangir. Just before the festival of Divali in 1619, Jehangir decided to release him. Guru Har Gobind refused to leave the prison unless 52 Hindu princes were released with him. Jehangir said that Guru Har Gobind must leave through a very narrow gate, only wide enough for one man to squeeze through. As many of the princes as could hold on to his cloak could go with him. The Guru had long cords fastened on to his cloak, so that all the princes could hold on. Everyone was freed.

SIKH LIFE 1

This section tells you something about what Sikhs believe about how they should live.

All Sikhs who are members of the Khalsa try to live their lives so that they are as much like the Gurus as possible. They believe that they should live honestly and work hard for what they earn. They should care for other people, as the Gurus did, because this is the best way to worship God. Gambling and stealing are forbidden, and so is adultery (sexual relationships outside of marriage). Sikhs are expected to show respect for all living things. They do not have to be vegetarian, but no Sikh should eat meat from an animal that has been killed in a way they consider cruel. Most Sikhs do not eat beef. This comes from respect for Hindus, who believe that the cow is a sacred animal.

Equality

It is an important part of Sikh teaching that everyone is equal. God's love is for everyone, so no one is better than anyone else. They also say that you cannot love God if you do not care about others, because God made everyone. This explains why Sikh teaching says that men and women and people from different backgrounds should always be treated in the same way.

Sewa

Sewa is an important part of life as a Sikh. It means "service," or helping others. The Guru Granth Sahib says "there is no worship without good deeds." The point of sewa is to worship God by helping others. For some Sikhs, this may mean giving money to help others. Guru Gobind Singh said that, if they could, Sikhs should give a tenth of their income to help other people. However, Sikhs accept that this is not always possible. In any case, if someone has a lot of money, it may mean more if they give some of their time instead.

Sewa can take many forms. It may mean doing jobs like cleaning the gurdwara, or helping to prepare or serve the langar, or caring for people who are ill. Often the jobs are things that people do not like doing. It is important to notice that sewa should not just be helping other Sikhs. Help should be offered to anyone who needs it, no matter who he or she is. An important part of sewa is talking to people about God, but Sikhs do not think that it is right to try to persuade people to become followers of Sikhism. Guru Nanak spent a lot of time talking to Hindus and Muslims, but he did not tell them they were wrong. What he did say was that what you believe is far more important than going through the ceremonies of a religion without really thinking about it.

Preparing and serving the langar is part of sewa.

34

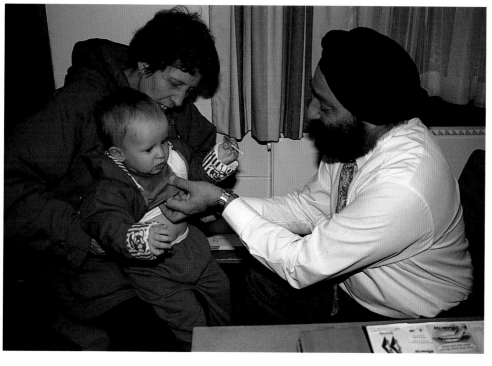

A Sikh doctor practicing in a Western country.

Medicine

Sikhs have always believed that it is important to care for people who are ill. There are stories about how Guru Nanak healed lepers. Lepers are people who suffered from a terrible skin disease that, in those days, had no cure, and that people were very afraid of. Many Sikhs today become doctors or nurses. In India, medical care is often not available to people who are poor. Clinics at gurdwaras, where people can be treated and given the drugs they need free of charge, help to fill the needs of the poor.

NEW WORD

Sewa Service, or helping others.

THE IMPORTANCE OF SEWA

This passage shows how important Sikhs think it is to serve others.

The hands of the gurmukh (true Sikh) are blessed, for they toil in the service of God and the sangat (Sikh community). They fetch water, grind corn, and perform any service that is required of them. They copy the compositions of the Gurus, pre-pare hymn books, and sing to the accompaniment of musical instruments. They bow low to the Guru and embrace their fellow-believers with joy. They labor to earn an honest living and distribute part of their income for the benefit of others. Ego and pride have been lost through serving others.

Bhai Gurdas Var 6 : 12

SIKH LIFE II

This section tells you about some ways Sikhs follow their religion in their lives.

Meditation

Sikhs are expected to spend time reading and thinking about the Gurus and their teachings. Thinking deeply about God is called meditation. Many Sikhs spend time every day meditating and repeating God's name. They also believe that reading the holy books is very important. The Guru Granth Sahib has been translated into other languages, but many Sikhs learn gurmukhi so that they can read it in the language that it was first written in. There are classes in the gurdwara to teach children gurmukhi.

Defending the religion

Guru Gobind Singh said that Sikhs should live their lives ready to defend their religion. This

There are classes at the gurdwara to teach gurmukhi.

means they should not use anything that might make them less able to fight against things that are wrong if this becomes necessary. For this reason, Sikhs are not supposed to drink alcohol or smoke tobacco. They should not use any drugs except for medical reasons. Guru Gobind Singh also told Sikhs that they needed to be prepared to fight for what is right. Although Sikhs believe that violence is wrong, they also believe that if something is unjust, it must be made fair. If all peaceful ways have failed, fighting may be the only way. This is why one of the symbols of Sikhism is a sword.

Turbans

A turban is a piece of cloth about 16 feet (5 m) long that is wound tightly around the head and tucked in to keep it in place. At the time of Guru Gobind Singh, many important people in India wore turbans as a sign of power. The Guru wore one as a sign of the power of the Sikhs. His followers copied him, and this is one reason why many Sikh men wear turbans today.

How to tie a turban.

Some women wear turbans, but this is not as common. The turban has become an important symbol of the Sikh faith, and Sikhs should not wear anything else on their heads.

In some countries, there have been problems over the wearing of turbans. Uniforms that have caps or helmets need to be changed so that Sikhs can wear turbans instead. There were particular problems in Great Britain in 1972, when the government passed a law that said that anyone riding a motorcycle had to wear a crash helmet. For several years, Sikhs argued that this was a law that they could not obey. Some Sikhs felt that it was so important they chose to go to prison rather than give up their turbans. It took until 1976 for the law to be changed to give Sikhs the right to wear turbans instead of crash helmets. In 1989, a new Employment Act in Great Britain gave Sikhs the right to wear a turban instead of a hard hat on some building sites.

GURU NANAK AND BHAI LALO

The importance of the way people live is shown in this Sikh story.

It is said that Guru Nanak was once invited to a rich man's house for a meal. Instead, he went to the house of a poor man called Bhai Lalo. The rich man was very annoyed, so Guru Nanak went to his house. He squeezed a piece of bread from the rich man's table, and a piece he had brought from Bhai Lalo's. Drops of milk came from Bhai Lalo's bread, but drops of blood came from the rich man's. Guru Nanak said that this was because Bhai Lalo was honest, even though he was poor, but the rich man had made his money by taking advantage of other people.

THE SIKH FAMILY

This section tells you something about the way Sikh families live.

Sikhs believe that family life is very important. They say that the best way for children to learn about the religion is for them to be taught about it at home. In India where Sikhism began, most people live in **extended families**. All the family —grandparents, aunts, uncles, cousins, in addition to parents and children—live either in the same house or very close to each other. Brothers and sisters and cousins may be thought of in exactly the same way. The way that parents and older people are treated is very important. They have had more life experience, and so they should be respected.

In the past, Sikh parents often made important decisions on behalf of their children. This included choosing the person they should marry. This is called an **arranged marriage**. Marriage joins two families, so Sikhs feel that it is a decision that should be made by the families as well as the couple themselves. This means that everyone can be sure the partners are suitable. Arranged marriages are not usually as strict as they used to be. In the past, the couple never met until their wedding day. Today, young people often suggest a person they know, and the couple usually meets— though not alone—at least a few times. The marriage cannot take place if the couple does not agree to it. Many young Sikhs prefer to leave such an important decision to their parents, but it sometimes causes problems for Sikhs who have been brought up in Western countries. They see friends with boyfriends or girlfriends, and feel that they should be allowed to choose their partner freely, too.

Women in Sikhism

Sikhism began when Hinduism and Islam were the two main religions in India. Guru Nanak said that these two religions treated women as if they were not as good as men, and this was wrong. He said that even the most powerful man owes his life to his mother, so men should respect women. God is in women just as much as in men. From the beginning of Sikhism, Guru Nanak taught that women should be equal in every way.

A Sikh family in a Western city.

Women often lead the worship in the gurdwara.

There are stories in Sikh history about women who became soldiers and were as important as men in fighting battles for the religion. In worship, women have always been treated in exactly the same way as men. Women who wish to become full members of the Sikh community take part in the amrit ceremony, and they are expected to wear the five K's, although many Sikh women do not wear a turban. In the gurdwara, women can take part in and lead services, and read from the Guru Granth Sahib. Men and women usually sit separately in the gurdwara, but this is because it is the custom in India in places where people are likely to be very close together. It is not part of the religion. Karah parshad and the langar are prepared and served by both men and women, and eaten together, and this helps to show that everyone is equal. Sikh women do not often take their name from their father or their husband because they are always called Kaur. For example, a typical name for a Sikh woman might be Jasbinder Kaur or Surjit Kaur.

NEW WORDS

Arranged marriage A marriage in which partners are suggested or chosen by relatives.
Extended family Grandparents, cousins, and other relatives living as one family.

GURU NANAK'S TEACHING ABOUT WOMEN

At the time of Guru Nanak, women were thought to be little more than possessions who could be controlled by men. This passage shows how different Guru Nanak's teaching was.

> *It is by woman that we are conceived,*
>
> *And from her that we are born.*
>
> *It is with her that we are betrothed and married.*
>
> *It is woman that we befriend, it is she who keeps the race going.*
>
> *Why should we call her inferior, who gives birth to great men?*
>
> *A woman is born of a woman, none is born without a woman.*

Adi Granth 473

SIKHS IN THE UNITED STATES

This section tells you something about Sikhs in the United States.

There are more than 300,000 Sikhs living in the U.S. today. Many more live in Canada. The first Sikhs to come to this country came to Yuba City, California, in 1846. Most Sikhs still live on the West Coast, although many live in major cities on the East Coast, like New York. A great number of Sikhs came to this country from 1967 to 1972. Sikhs now living in the United States were born here. There are many differences between life in the Punjab and life in the U.S. and some Sikhs find these differences difficult to accept. Most Sikhs feel at home in the U.S., but they are very proud of their background and do not want it to be forgotten.

Most Sikhs feel at home in Western countries.

Language

Many Sikhs now living in the U.S. are the children of American Sikhs and have never been to India. They may not speak much Punjabi, and this can make it difficult to understand the religion fully. It can also make it difficult to follow services in the gurdwara. Some gurdwaras now hold at least some of their services in English, so that people who do not speak very good Punjabi can join in. Many children go to special classes at the gurdwara, so that they can learn Punjabi and gurmukhi.

Gurdwaras

Wherever there is a group of Sikhs, there will be a gurdwara. There are at least 50, or perhaps as many as 90, gurdwaras in the U.S., but most were not specially built. Some are in houses or other buildings that Sikhs have bought and made into gurdwaras. In India, gurdwaras are usually open all day everyday, and there is no particular day that Sikhs are expected to go there. In the U.S., it is often more convenient to hold services in the gurdwara on Saturday or Sunday, because this fits into the way of life in the U.S. Weddings are usually held in gurdwaras, although in India they are held in the open air. Many gurdwaras in the U.S. have also become important meeting places, especially for older Sikhs who have retired from work.

Converts

Sikhism does not have **missionaries**. A missionary is someone who goes out to tell other people about their religion. Sikhs believe that their religion is the best for them, but they do not try to persuade other people to follow it. They accept that it is possible to find God in other religions and believe that it is important to try to see God in every person. Guru Nanak preached to people of different religions and welcomed them. Sikhism is a very open religion and anyone is welcome to go to the gurdwara for a service and to share in the langar. Of course, everyone who attends is

Learning about other people's beliefs is important.

expected to be respectful and take off their shoes, cover their head, and make sure they are not carrying tobacco. The way that Sikhs live has earned respect, and many people who were not born Sikhs have become interested in the religion. Some have decided that they want to live their lives following its teaching, and a number of people in the U.S. have now **converted** to Sikhism.

NEW WORDS

Convert To become a member of a religion.

Missionary Someone who travels to tell other people about their religion.

AKAL USTAT

This passage is from a hymn called Akal Ustat, which means "The praise of the eternal one." It shows the openness of the Sikh religion.

Humanity is one race in the whole world. God as creator, as bountiful and as merciful is one God. We should never try to divide God into

the God of different groups. Worship the one God, the one divine teacher of everyone. Everyone has the same human form, everyone has the same soul.

Dasam Granth.

SPECIAL OCCASIONS I

This section tells you about special things that happen to young Sikhs.

Birth

As soon as possible after a baby is born, someone repeats the **Mool Mantar**. This is the beginning of the Guru Granth Sahib and it sums up the most important things that Sikhs believe. It means that the first things that a baby hears are the most important Sikh beliefs. Parents may share their joy at the birth by giving candy, sweet foods, or other small presents to friends and neighbors. It is the custom for relations to visit soon after the birth and give presents for the baby.

The naming ceremony

The naming ceremony is often part of a normal service at the gurdwara. It usually takes place within a few weeks of the baby's birth, although it can be later. The parents take the baby to the gurdwara, and other relations meet there too. They are there to thank God for the

Parents often give a new cover for the Guru Granth Sahib at the naming ceremony.

new baby, and to choose its name. (Many babies already have a nickname that has been used before the official name is given.) It is the custom for parents to take with them a **rumala** (a length of cloth used for covering the Guru Granth Sahib when it is not being read). They also pay for the Karah parshad that everyone shares at the end of the service.

At the end of the service, there is the usual prayer called the Ardas. When a baby is being welcomed, this prayer includes the names of the parents, and thanks God for the gift of the baby. At the end of the prayer, the parents go to the front of the gurdwara, and lay the baby on the floor in front of the Guru Granth Sahib. Then the Guru Granth Sahib is opened at random. This means that the granthi opens it without choosing a particular page. He or she reads the first new verse on the left-hand page. Then he or she tells the parents the letter of the alphabet that began the first word of the verse. The baby's name will begin with this letter. For example, if the letter was J, it could be a name like *Jaswinder* or *Jaswant* or *Jarnail*. If the baby is a boy, he will also have the name Singh, and if a girl, she will have the name Kaur. When the parents have chosen the name, the granthi announces it to the congregation, and says, "Jo bole so nihal." (This cannot clearly be translated into English.) The congregation shouts "Sat sri akal" (God is truth) to show their agreement. Then everyone shares the Karah parshad, a special dessert, and congratulates the new parents.

Sikhs often use the same first names for both boys and girls, so the name Singh or Kaur is often the only way of telling by their name whether a Sikh is male or female. Some Sikhs use Singh and Kaur as their family name, or surname, but others use their real family name as well. For example, a Sikh man might be called Jarnail Singh Grewal.

PEOPLE

A naming ceremony.

Sometimes, when the baby has been given its name, there is an extra ceremony in which the baby is given amrit. (This may already have taken place at home.) The granthi places a few drops of amrit on its tongue. The mother drinks the rest. Prayers are said, asking that the baby will have a long life and asking God's blessing on him or her. The granthi may also give the baby its first kara—the steel bangle that is one of the five K's. Tiny ones are made for babies. This kara is then replaced as the child grows.

HYMN FOR THE NAMING CEREMONY

This hymn was written by the mother of Guru Arjan when he was born. It is often used at Sikh naming ceremonies today.

> Dear son, this is your mother's blessing. May God never be out of your mind even for a moment. Meditation on God should be your constant concern. It purges people from [of] all faults. May God the Guru be kind to you. May you love the company of God's people. May God robe you with honor and may your food be the singing of God's praises.

Adi Granth 486

NEW WORD

Mool Mantar Beginning of the Guru Granth Sahib.

Rumala Cloth used for covering the Guru Granth Sahib.

43

SPECIAL OCCASIONS II

This section tells you about Sikh teachings on marriage.

Marriage

Sikhs are encouraged to marry, and marriage is called **anand karaj,** which means "the ceremony of happiness." The Gurus taught that family life was very important and being married is thought to be a necessary part of this. Many Sikh weddings are arranged marriages, and even if the couple have suggested their marriage, the families will still be very involved. The bride should be at least 18 years old, and it is usual for the groom to be older than the bride. A marriage cannot take place unless both the bride and groom agree to it.

Sikh weddings usually take place in the morning. They must always take place in the presence of the Guru Granth Sahib. In India, they may be held in the open air or in a large tent. In the West they are usually held in the gurdwara. Any Sikh may perform the marriage ceremony, provided that he or she has been chosen by both families.

On the evening before the wedding, the bride's friends and female relatives may meet at her house. They have a party where she is given money and special sweet foods. They paint beautiful patterns on her hands and feet with a special dye that will last for several days.

On the morning of the wedding, the bridegroom and his relatives are welcomed to the bride's house, where they are given refreshments. Often presents are exchanged, usually things like lengths of cloth for turbans or clothing. Then they all go to the gurdwara. The bridegroom usually wears a red or pink turban and has a scarf around his neck. He sits at the front, in front of the Guru Granth Sahib. The bride's father puts a garland of flowers on the Guru Granth Sahib. The bride enters with her sister or other female relative. She wears red, often with beautiful gold jewelry. After bowing to the Guru Granth Sahib as usual, she sits next to the bridegroom, and is given a garland of flowers by her father.

The couple and their parents stand while prayers are said asking God's blessing on the marriage. A passage from the Guru Granth Sahib is read, and the person leading the service gives a talk about marriage and what it means. The couple is asked if they understand and accept their responsibilities to each other as husband and wife. When they have nodded their agreement, the bride's father gives her one end of the bridegroom's scarf. This is a symbol

The bride and groom are given gifts of money.

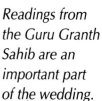

Readings from the Guru Granth Sahib are an important part of the wedding.

that they are being joined together as husband and wife. The bride holds the scarf for the rest of the ceremony.

The most important part of the ceremony follows. This is the reading of the **Lavan**, a hymn written for weddings by Guru Ram Das. It has four verses, which are spoken one at a time and then sung. Each verse explains something about marriage. As each verse is sung, the bride and groom walk in a clockwise direction around the Guru Granth Sahib. When they have done this for the fourth time, they are married. Everyone stands to join in the Ardas prayer, and there may be speeches before everyone shares the Karah parshad. A meal follows, which may be held in the langar room.

Divorce

If a couple has problems in their marriage, both families will do their best to solve the problems. If the marriage cannot be saved, divorce is allowed, and either person may marry again in the gurdwara.

THE LAVAN (WEDDING HYMN)

The Lavan has four verses. Each one compares the love of men and women with the love of a soul for God. This is part of the fourth verse, which is about perfect love.

As the fourth round begins, our spirits find peace, for God enters our hearts and minds. Through the Guru's grace, we know God's presence, and the sweetness of God spreads through our souls and bodies. This sweetness comes from God's love, which keeps all who speak God's name so that they may live in bliss.

Guru Ram Das

NEW WORDS

Anand karaj Sikh wedding ceremony.
Lavan Wedding hymn.

SPECIAL OCCASIONS III

This section explains what happens when a Sikh dies.

Sikh teaching about death

Sikhs do not believe that death is the end. They believe in **reincarnation**. This is the belief that when you die your soul moves on to another body. This happens over and over again. Sikhs believe that they have lived other lives, in which they were not human beings, but they believe that only human beings are capable of knowing and loving God. Guru Nanak said that only reincarnation explains the unfairness of life, because the things you have done in a past life can follow you and affect this life. This goes on until, with God's help, you become close enough to God to break out of the rebirth cycle. Then you will not be reborn, but will live with God forever.

Sikhs say that death is no different from going to sleep. Just as you go to sleep when you are tired, and wake up ready for another day, so at the end of life you die and are reborn. Death is the end of one life, but the beginning of another one. They say that it is natural for people who are left to feel sorrow, but they should also remember that the person who has died has gone on to another life.

Sikh funerals

After a person has died, the body is washed by relatives of the same sex, and dressed in the five K's. Then it is wrapped in a white sheet. A Sikh who has died is always cremated, which means the body is burned. In India, this takes place on the day of death, and the body is placed on a special **funeral pyre**, often on the bank of a river. In the West, the funeral takes place as soon as possible after the death, and the body is taken to a **crematorium**. Male relatives usually help to put the body in the incinerator, in the same way that in India they would help to lift it on to the funeral pyre.

The most important prayer at the funeral is the **Sohila**, which is the prayer said by every Sikh before going to sleep at night. This helps to remind people that death is like sleep. After the body has been burned, the ashes are usually scattered on running water. This may be the ocean or a river. Some Western Sikhs have the ashes flown back to the Punjab so that the ashes can be scattered there.

The funeral is often followed by a service at the gurdwara. This includes the singing of hymns, the Ardas prayer, and the giving of Karah parshad, as well as a langar. Sometimes there is an Akhand Path at the gurdwara, or there may be a reading of the Guru Granth Sahib all the way through at the home of the person who has died. This is done by the relatives and is called a Sadharan Path. It is not an Akhand Path

A Sikh funeral in a European country.

because the readers will have to return to their normal jobs during the day, and so it is not non-stop. It is read early in the morning and in the evening. Sikhs believe that reading the Guru Granth Sahib like this gives comfort to the relatives of someone who has died.

Male relatives help to carry the coffin.

NEW WORDS

Crematorium Place where bodies are burned after death.
Funeral pyre Special fire for burning a dead body.
Reincarnation Belief in rebirth after death.
Sohila Sikh bedtime prayer.

Sikhs do not put up any headstones or other memorials to people who have died. They believe that the good things that someone did during their life should be the way they are remembered, rather than the memory of the person being based on a stone memorial. Stones are also forbidden to make sure that the memorial does not become a place for worship.

KIRTAN SOHILA

The Kirtan Sohila is the bedtime prayer that all Sikhs should pray before they go to sleep. It is also used at funerals. This is part of it.

Worldly souls who scorn God's sweetness suffer pain because of their conceit. The thorn of death pricks deeper and deeper. Those who love God's sacred name shall break the bonds of birth and death. Thus they find the eternal One; thus they win supreme honor. I am poor and humble, keep and save me, God most high. Grant the aid that your name can give me. Grant me the peace and joy. Grant the joy of serving all who praise God's name.

Adi Granth 13

INDEX

The numbers in **bold** tell where the main definitions of the words are.